Sante D'Orazio
Polaroids

Sante D'Orazio
Polaroids

Text by Glenn O'Brien

Schirmer/Mosel

Legends (Polaroids) by Sante D'Orazio

Sante D'Orazio is a photographer and artist whose diverse career has embraced fashion, portraiture, erotica, photography-based fine art, and painting. Trained as a painter, he picked up a camera as a young man in the 1980s and quickly became known for his distinctive work in fashion, producing editorial work for elite magazines such as *Vogue*, *Esquire* and *Vanity Fair*, while creating campaigns for some of the most important fashion and beauty brands including Versace, Valentino, Revlon, and L'Oréal, as well as innovating the visual identity of Victoria's Secret.

Fresh out of art school and mentoring by a famous street photographer Lou Bernstein, D'Orazio soon found himself surrounded by the first generation known as "supermodels," and his pictures, marked by their uniquely intimate rapport with his subjects, were instrumental in establishing the legendary status of such women as Christy Turlington, Cindy Crawford, Naomi Campbell, Kristen McMenamy, Linda Evangelista, Georgina Grenville, Eva Herzigova, Claudia Schiffer, Helena Christensen, Jamie King, and Kate Moss. What was his secret? In addition to possessing a classicist's eye, he seemed uniquely unafraid of the most attractive women in the world. Men tend to fear great beauties, but Sante doesn't. He enjoys them. He appreciates them. You could say that he is to gorgeous women what Siegfried & Roy are to tigers. A fearless friend, a sincere admirer, a mentor (and occasional ring master.)

D'Orazio's gift for maximizing the beauty of even the most beautiful people led to a portraiture practice that continues today. His subjects include Al Pacino, Johnny Depp, Sharon Stone, Catherine Zeta-Jones, Anthony Kiedis, Sean Penn, Arnold Schwarzenegger, Keith Richards, Roman Polanski, John Travolta, Susan Sarandon, and such artists as Jeff Koons, Damien Hirst, Francesco Clemente, Phillip Taaffe, Matthew Barney, Alex Katz, Julian Schnabel, Ed Ruscha, Nobuyoshi Araki, George Condo, and Maurizio Cattelan.

In shooting during the pre-digital age, D'Orazio, like most of his peers, took Polaroids to test exposure and composition. Portrait photography is a lot about ease in the moment. Finding a calm space in time where the personality can emerge. These Polaroids, usually made as a test of the light, show ease at that very first moment. They say, "see, relax, you look amazing."

Often these Polaroids have a special quality of light and tone that makes them extraordinary works in their own right. Perhaps there's something about the casual, throwaway spirit of the shot itself that imparts a particularly poignant and unique spirit—as if the shot itself knew that it was one-of-a-kind, a true original.

How did the Bible put it? "The stone the builders rejected has become the cornerstone." Not that any of these extraordinary test shots was rejected, but they are remarkable, unique byproducts of evanescent moods, captured moments of magic that often outshine the intended work.

Glenn O'Brien

LEGENDS (POLAROIDS) VON SANTE D'ORAZIO

Sante D'Orazio ist ein Photograph und Künstler, dessen breitgefächerte Karriere Mode, Portrait, Erotica, Photokunst und Malerei umfasst. Als junger Mann nahm der studierte Maler in den 1980er Jahren eine Kamera in die Hand und war schon bald für seine unverwechselbare Modephotographie bekannt, mit redaktionellen Beiträgen für Elite-Magazine wie *Vogue*, *Esquire* und *Vanity Fair*, mit Werbekampagnen für einige der bedeutendsten Mode- und Kosmetik-Marken wie Versace, Valentino, Revlon und L'Oréal und dem neuen Look, den er für Victoria's Secret entwickelte.

Kaum hatte er das Kunststudium und die Lehrzeit bei Lou Bernstein, einem berühmten Street Photographer, hinter sich, war D'Orazio bereits von der ersten Generation der „Supermodels" umgeben, und seine Bilder, die sich durch besondere Intimität zwischen dem Photographen und seinen Modellen auszeichnen, waren maßgeblich am legendären Status von Frauen wie Christy Turlington, Cindy Crawford, Naomi Campbell, Kristen McMenamy, Linda Evangelista, Georgina Grenville, Eva Herzigova, Claudia Schiffer, Helena Christensen, Jamie King und Kate Moss beteiligt. Was war sein Geheimnis? Er besitzt nicht nur ein Kennerauge, offensichtlich ließ er sich von den attraktivsten Frauen der Welt auch nicht einschüchtern. Männer haben oft Angst vor schönen Frauen, nicht so Sante. Er genießt sie. Schätzt sie. Man könnte sagen, er ist für hinreißende Frauen, was Siegfried & Roy für Tiger sind. Ein furchtloser Freund, ein ehrlicher Bewunderer, ein Mentor (und gelegentlicher Dompteur).

D'Orazios Gabe, aus der Schönheit selbst der schönsten Menschen das Maximum herauszuholen, führte zu einer Portrait-Tätigkeit, die bis heute andauert. Er hat Al Pacino, Johnny Depp, Sharon Stone, Catherine Zeta-Jones, Anthony Kiedis, Sean Penn, Arnold Schwarzenegger, Keith Richards, Roman Polanski, John Travolta, Susan Sarandon portraitiert und Künstler wie Jeff Koons, Damien Hirst, Francesco Clemente, Phillip Taafe, Matthew Barney, Alex Katz, Julian Schnabel, Ed Ruscha, Nobuyoshi Araki, George Condo und Maurizio Cattelan.

Bei Shootings im prädigitalen Zeitalter machte D'Orazio, wie viele seiner Kollegen, Polaroids, um Belichtungszeit und Bildkomposition zu testen. In der Portraitphotographie geht es vor allem um Entspanntheit im Moment, darum, einen Ruhepol zu finden, an dem die Persönlichkeit zu Tage treten kann. Diese Polaroids, meist als Test fürs Licht entstanden, zeigen Entspanntheit in diesem allerersten Moment. Sie sagen, „na also, relax, du siehst toll aus."

Oft haben Licht und Farbigkeit auf diesen Polaroids ein spezielle Qualität, die sie zu eigenständigen Meisterwerken macht. Vielleicht liegt ja im beiläufigen Ex-und-hopp-Charakter selbst etwas, das der Aufnahme etwas besonders Pointiertes und Einzigartiges verleiht – als wisse die Aufnahme selbst, dass sie ein Unikat, ein echtes Original ist.

Wie heißt es in der Bibel? „Der Stein, den die Bauleute verworfen haben, ist zum Eckstein geworden." Nicht, dass eine dieser außergewöhnlichen Testaufnahmen verworfen wurde, aber sie sind bemerkenswerte, einmalige Nebenprodukte flüchtiger Stimmungen, festgehaltener magischer Momente, die das eigentliche Produkt oft in den Schatten stellen.

Glenn O'Brien

Legends (Polaroids) de Sante D'Orazio

Sante D'Orazio est un photographe et artiste dont la carrière diversifiée touche aussi bien à la mode, au portrait et à l'érotisme, qu'à la photo d'art et la peinture. Formé d'abord à la peinture, le jeune homme s'empare de l'appareil photo dans les années 1980 et se fait rapidement connaître par son travail hors pair dans le monde de la mode. Il contribue alors à des magazines haut de gamme tels que *Vogue*, *Esquire* ou *Vanity Fair*, et réalise des campagnes publicitaires pour certaines des marques les plus en vue de la mode et de la cosmétique – Versace, Valentino, Revlon, L'Oréal. Il crée également la nouvelle identité visuelle de Victoria's Secret.

Fraîchement sorti de l'école d'art et de sa formation auprès du célèbre *street* photographe Lou Bernstein, D'Orazio est bientôt lui-même entouré de la première génération de « supermodels ». Ses photos, empreintes de cette intimité unique qui caractérise son lien avec ses modèles, ont considérablement aidé à élever au rang de légendes des femmes comme Christy Turlington, Cindy Crawford, Naomi Campbell, Kristen McMenamy, Linda Evangelista, Georgina Grenville, Eva Herzigova, Claudia Schiffer, Helena Christensen, Jamie King et Kate Moss. Son secret ? Outre son regard expert, il semble avoir été singulièrement peu intimidé par les plus belles femmes du monde. Les hommes ont souvent peur devant tant de beauté féminine, Sante non. Il s'en réjouit, il la savoure. On pourrait dire qu'il est aux femmes sublimes ce que Siegfried & Roy sont aux tigres. Un ami sans crainte, un admirateur sincère, un mentor (et parfois dompteur).

Le don de D'Orazio de faire ressortir le maximum de beauté même des individus les plus beaux a instauré une pratique du portrait qui perdure encore aujourd'hui. Il a ainsi photographié Al Pacino, Johnny Depp, Sharon Stone, Catherine Zeta-Jones, Anthony Kiedis, Sean Penn, Arnold Schwarzenegger, Keith Richards, Roman Polanski, John Travolta, Susan Sarandon, et des artistes comme Jeff Koons, Damien Hirst, Francesco Clemente, Phillip Taaffe, Matthew Barney, Alex Katz, Julian Schnabel, Ed Ruscha, Nobuyoshi Araki, George Condo et Maurizio Cattelan.

Lors des shootings à l'ère pré-numérique, D'Orazio, comme la plupart de ses pairs, prenait d'abord des Polaroids pour tester le temps d'exposition et la composition d'ensemble. En photographie de portrait, beaucoup tient à l'état de détente du moment, il faut trouver un temps de repos qui permette à la personnalité d'émerger. Ces Polaroids, souvent effectués pour tester l'éclairage, montrent ce tout premier instant de détente, comme s'ils disaient : « Relax, tu es fantastique. »

Il y a dans ces Polaroids une lumière et une tonalité d'une qualité particulière qui fait d'eux des chefs-d'œuvre à part entière. Peut-être y a-t-il dans leur aspect fortuit, désinvolte, quelque chose qui donne au tirage son caractère unique et poignant – comme si le tirage lui-même savait son unicité, son authenticité.

Que lit-on dans la Bible déjà ? « La pierre qu'ont rejetée les bâtisseurs est devenue la pierre angulaire. » Non pas que la moindre de ces extraordinaires images test ait été rejetée, mais elles sont les uniques et remarquables produits résiduels d'ambiances fugaces, de moments de magie capturée, qui font de l'ombre au produit réel.

Glenn O'Brien

Polaroids

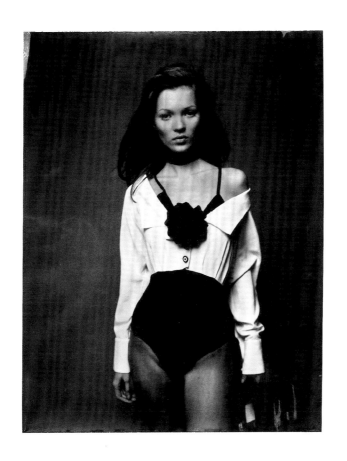

Kate Moss

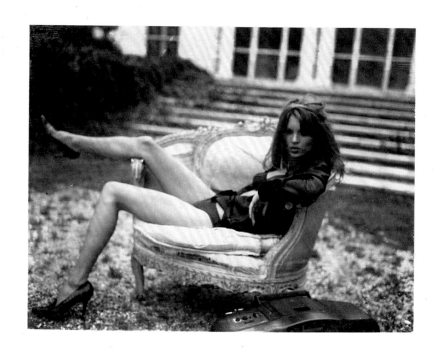

Kate Moss

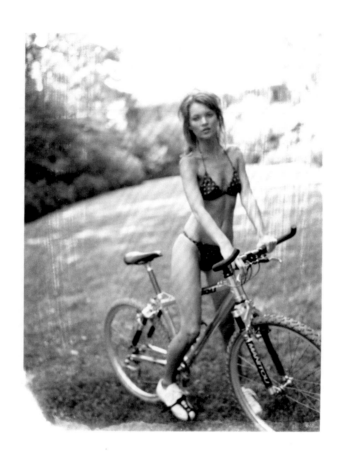

Kate Moss

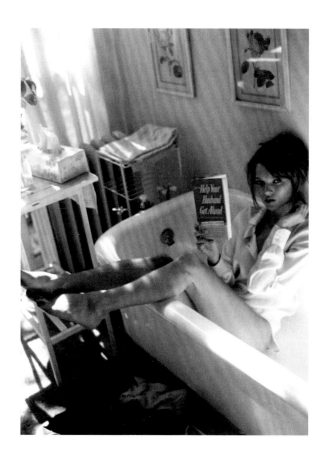

Kate Moss

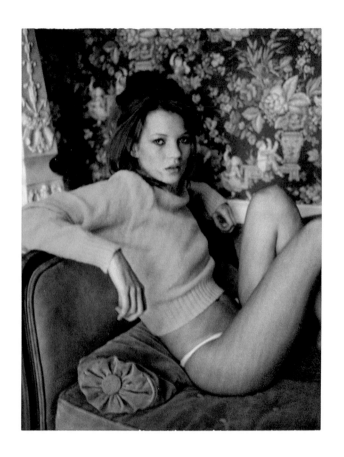

Kate Moss

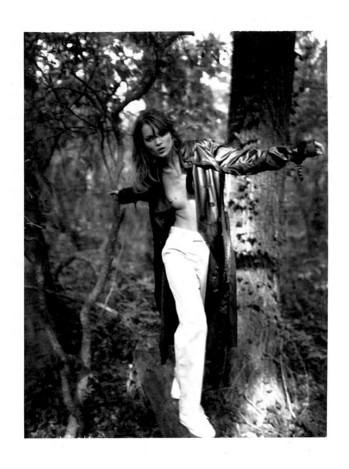

Kate Moss

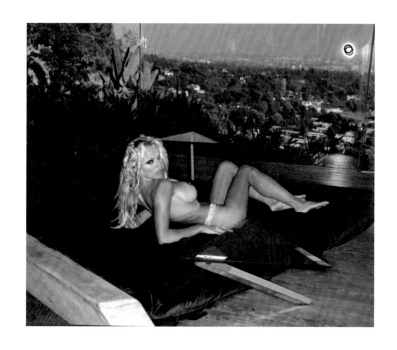

Pamela Anderson

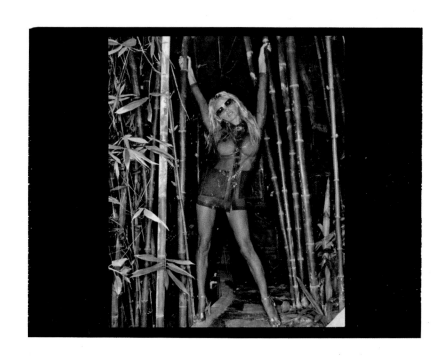

Pamela Anderson

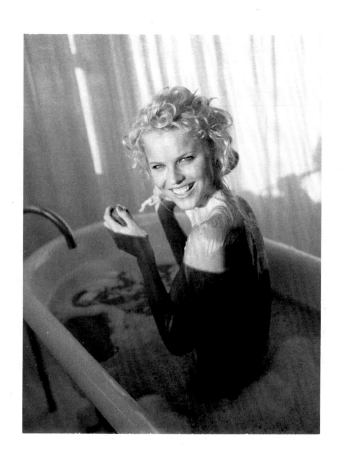

Eva Herzigova

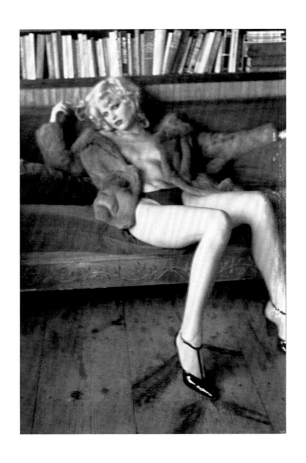

Eva Herzigova

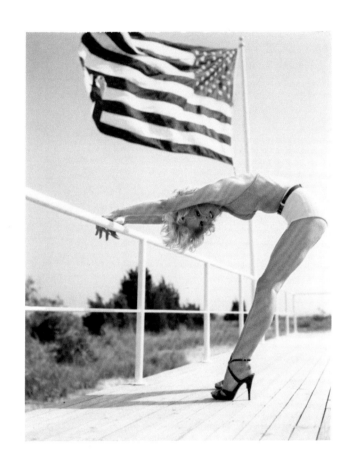

Eva Herzigova

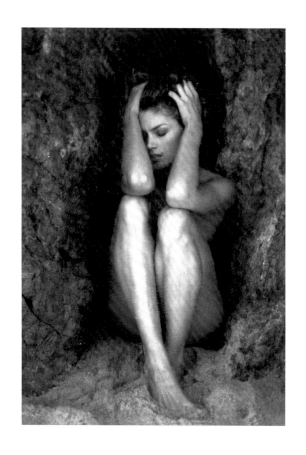

Cindy Crawford

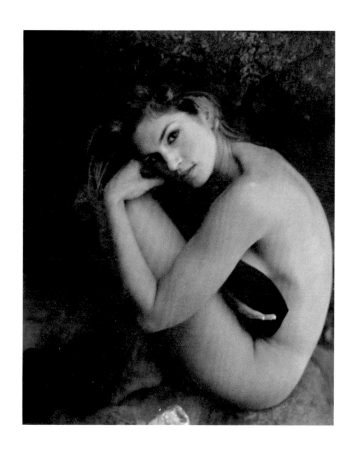

Cindy Crawford

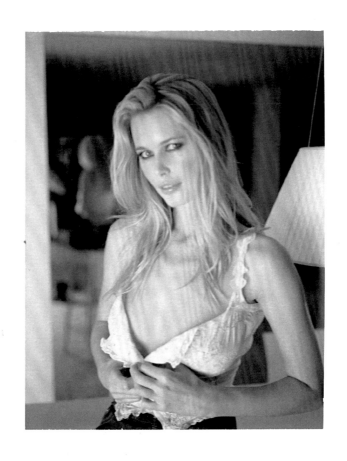

Claudia Schiffer

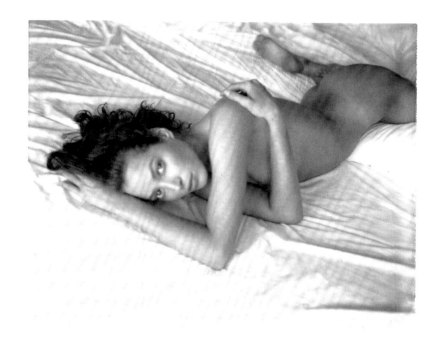

Christy Turlington

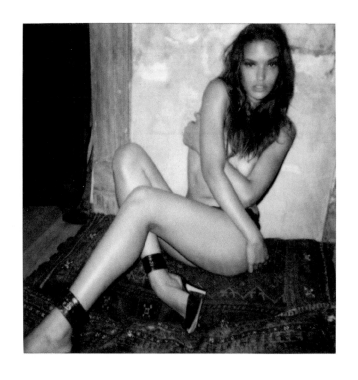

Kat Fonseca

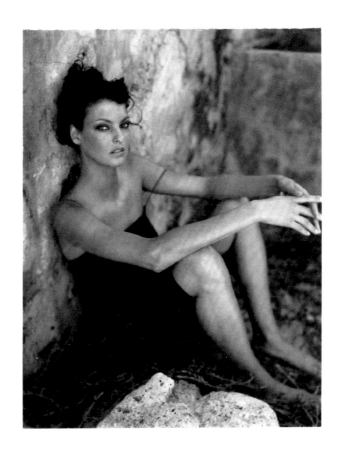

Linda Evangelista

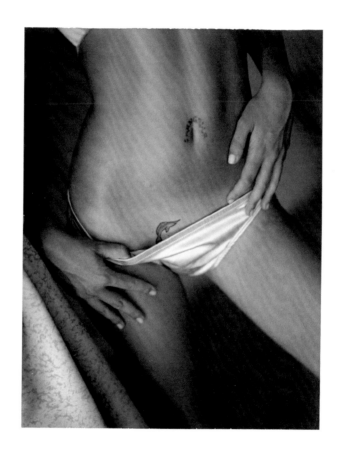

Georgina Grenville

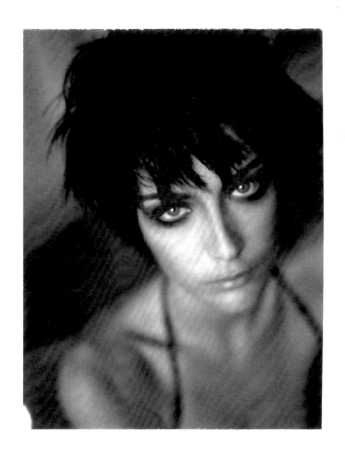

Georgina Grenville

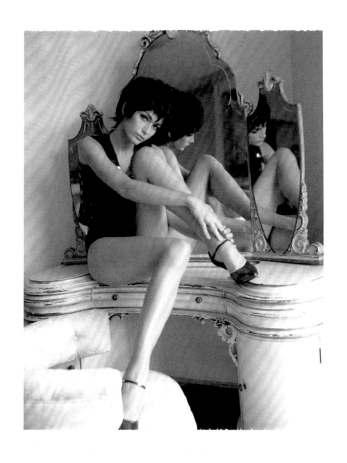

Georgina Grenville

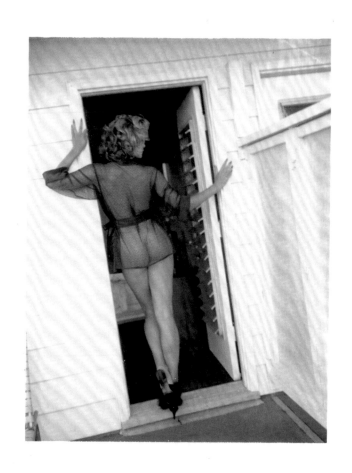

Rachel Williams

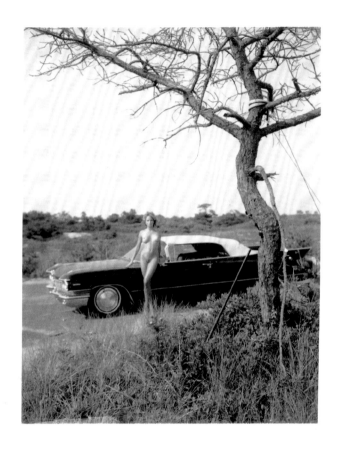

Rachel Williams

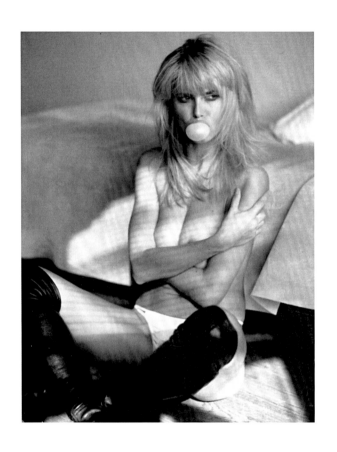

Heidi Klum

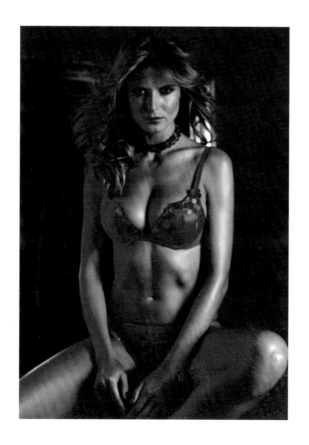

Heidi Klum

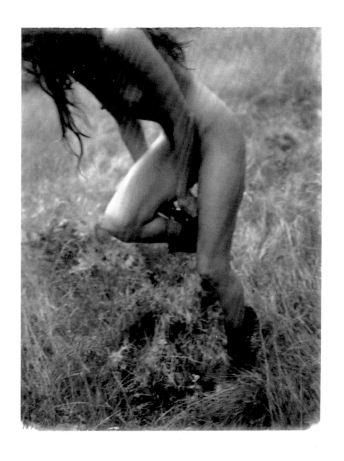

Tahnee Welch

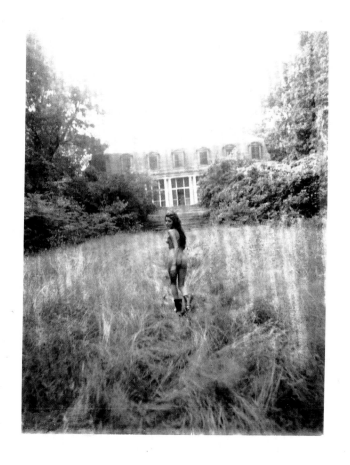

Tahnee Welch

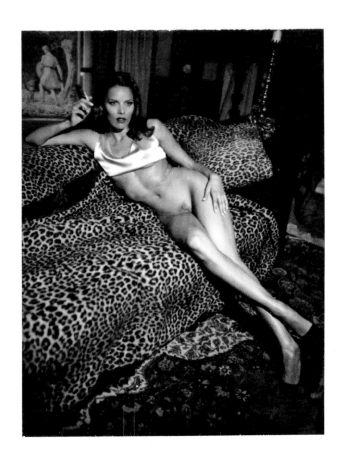

Tahnee Welch

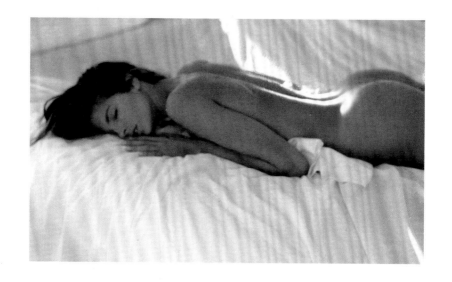

Stephanie Seymour

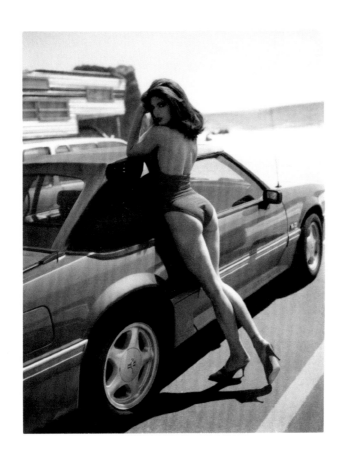

Stephanie Seymour

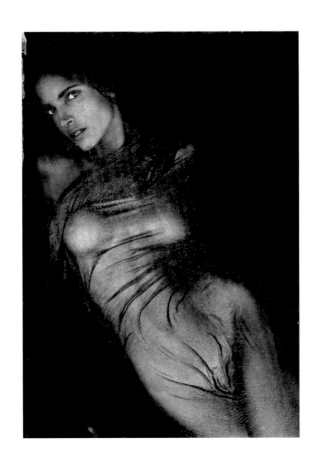

Stephanie Seymour

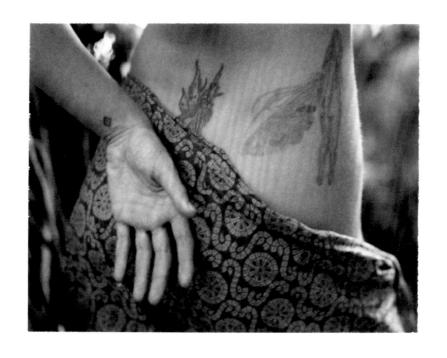

Jamie King

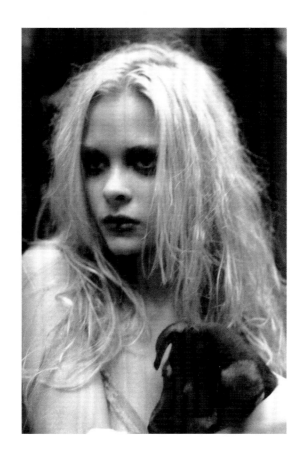

Jamie King

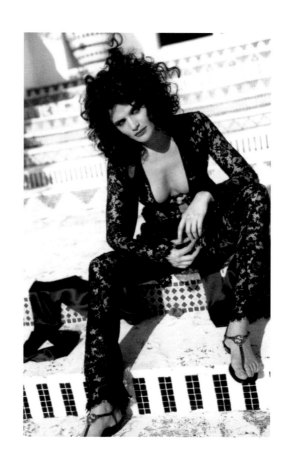

Helena Christensen

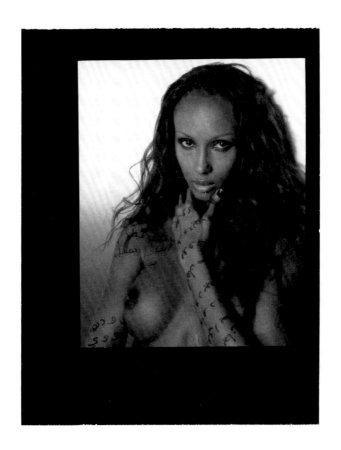

Iman

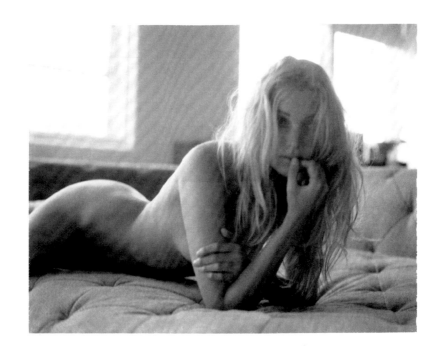

Elsa Hosk

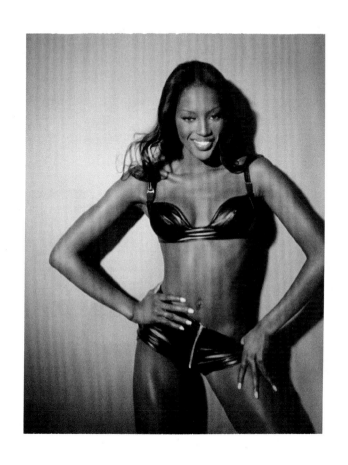

Naomi Campbell

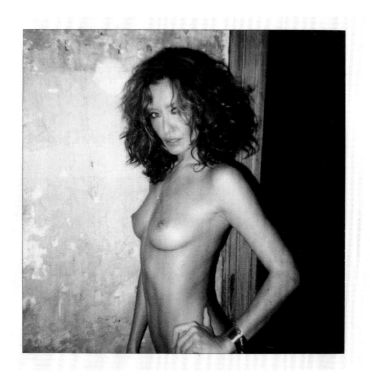

Sky Nellor

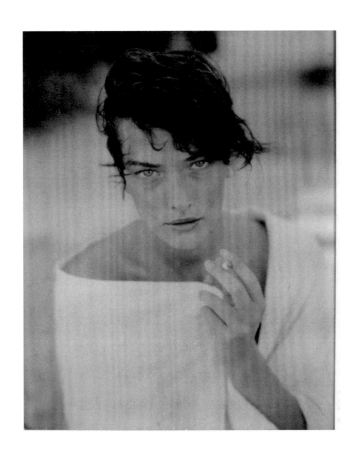

Tatjana Patitz

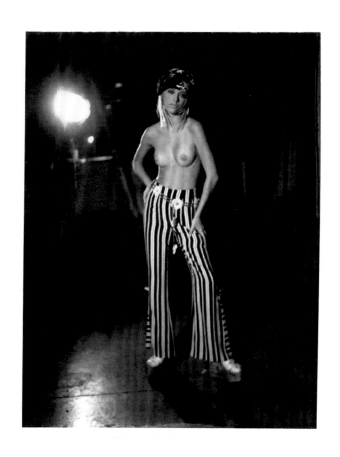

Leilani Dowding

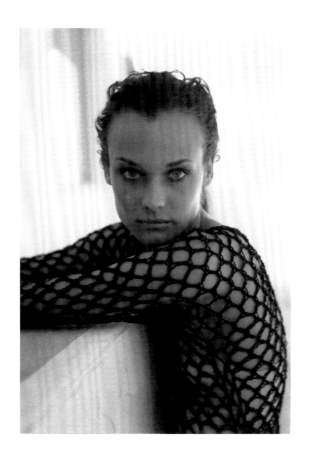

Amber Valletta

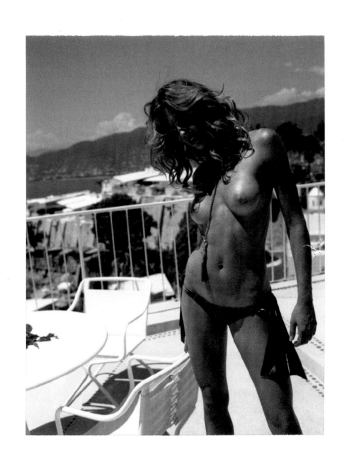

Tricia Helfer

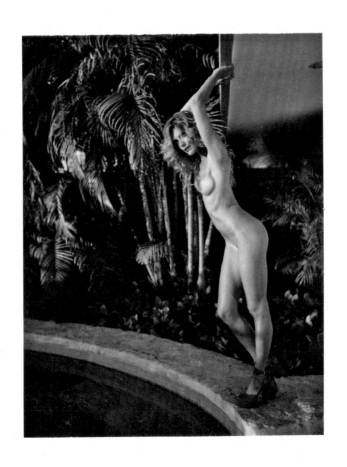

Tricia Helfer

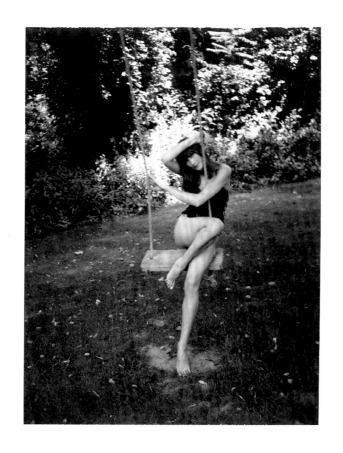

Carla Bruni

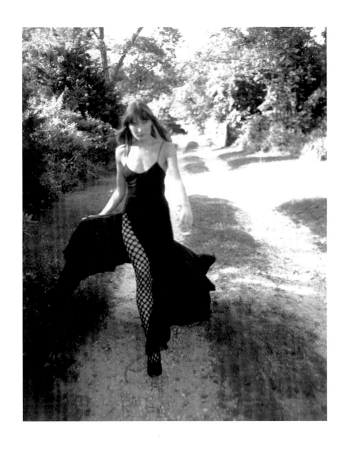

Carla Bruni

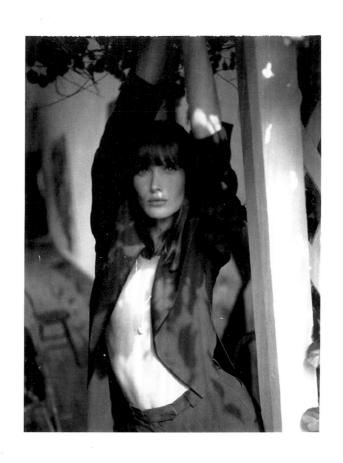

Carla Bruni

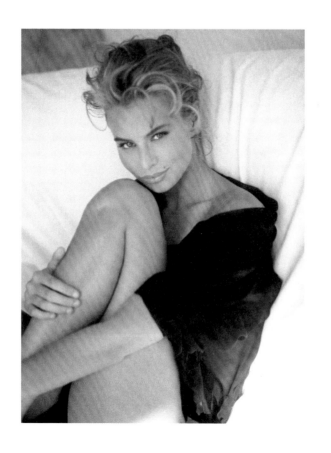

Niki Taylor

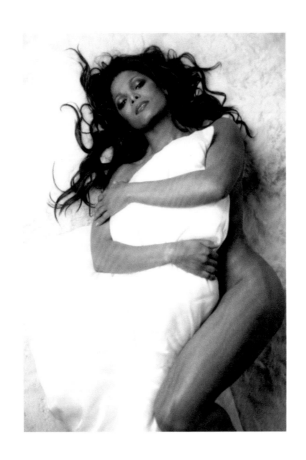

Janet Jackson

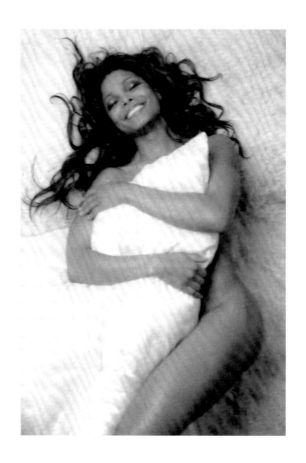

Janet Jackson

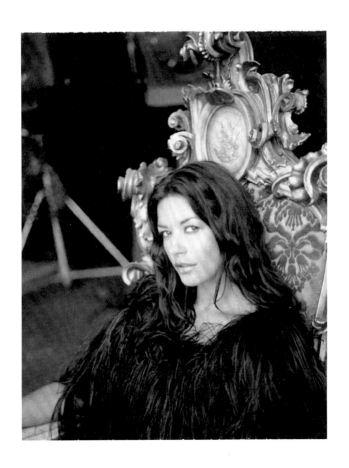

Catherine Zeta-Jones

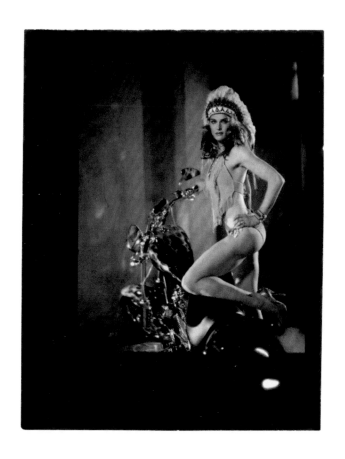

Brooke Shields

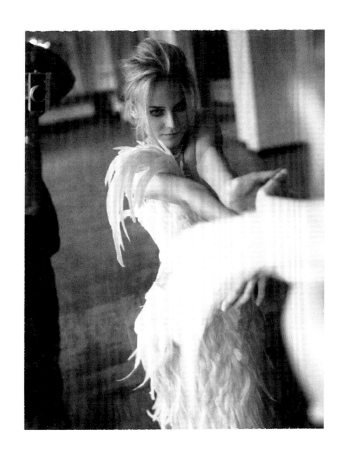

Diane Kruger

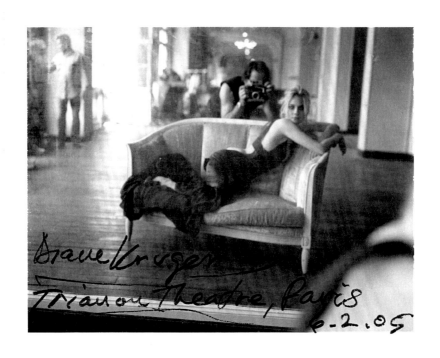

Diane Kruger

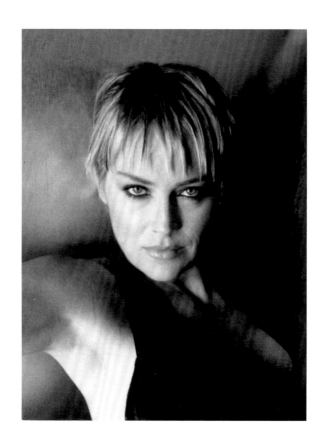

Sharon Stone

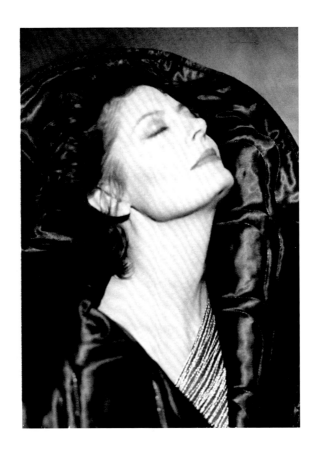

Susan Sarandon

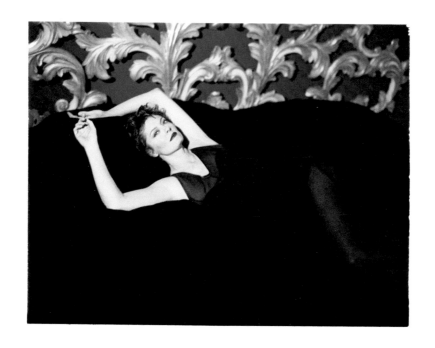

Susan Sarandon

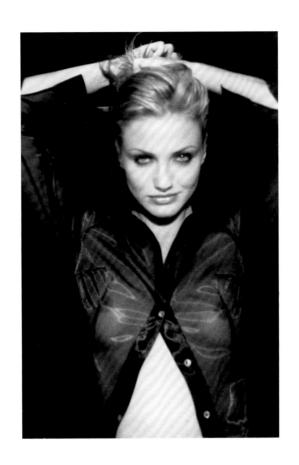

Cameron Diaz

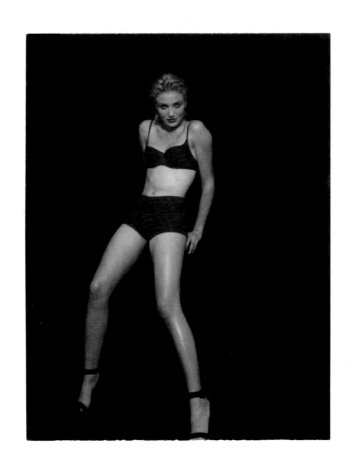

Cameron Diaz

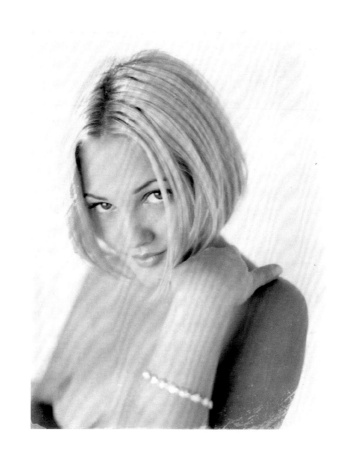

Drew Barrymore

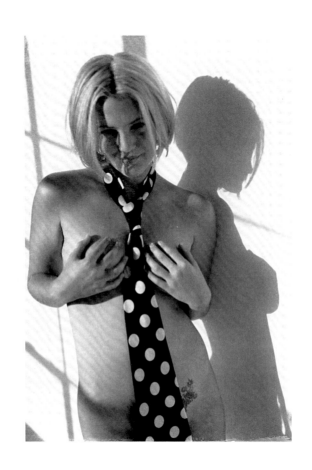

Drew Barrymore

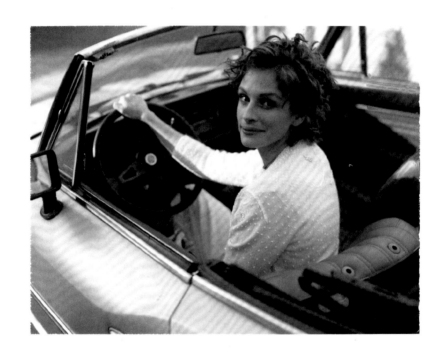

Julia Roberts

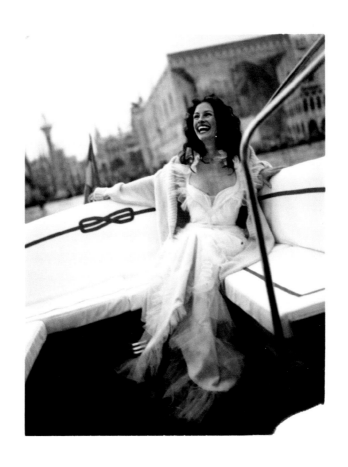

Julia Roberts

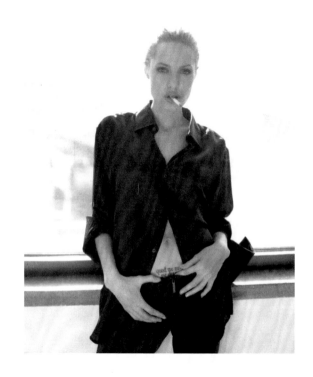

Angelina Jolie

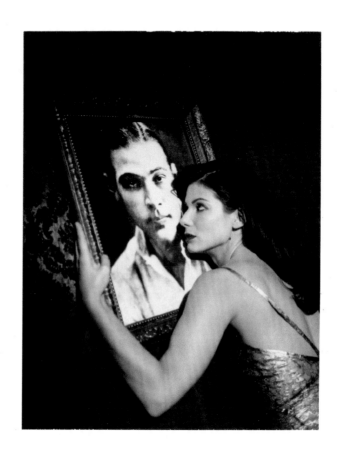

Sandra Bullock

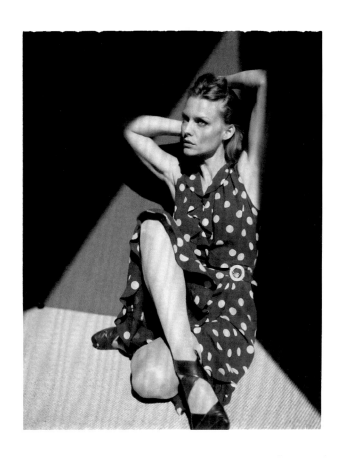

Michelle Pfeiffer

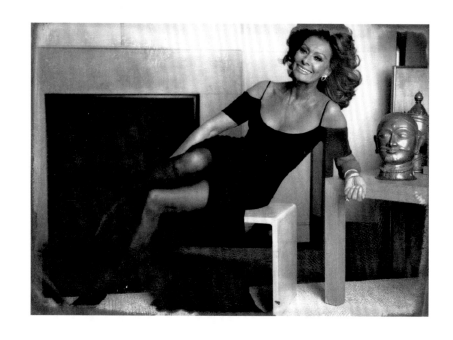

Sophia Loren

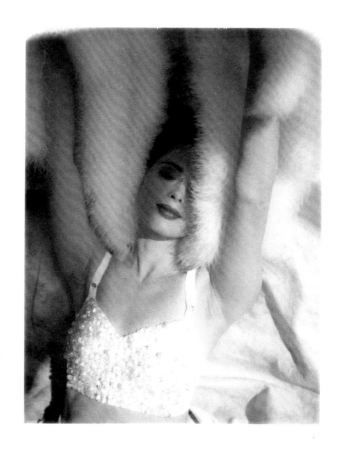

Isabella Rossellini

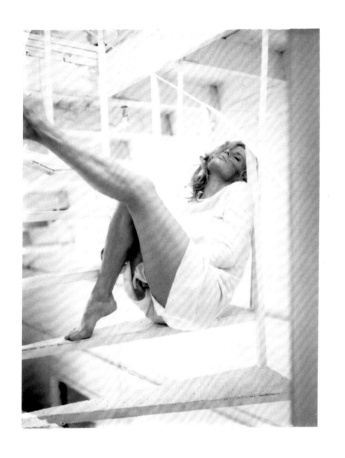

Kim Basinger

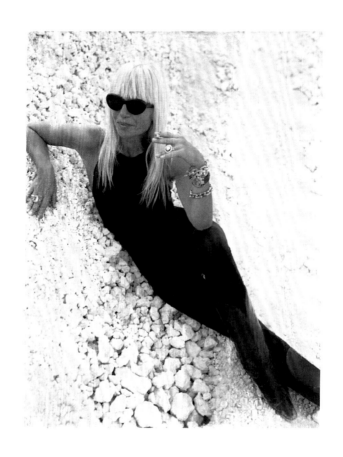

Donatella Versace

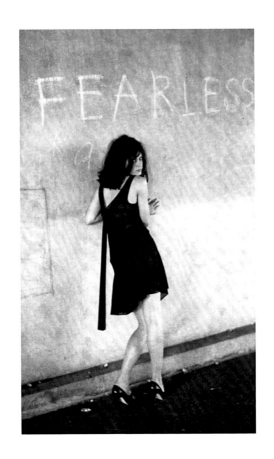

Linda Fiorentino

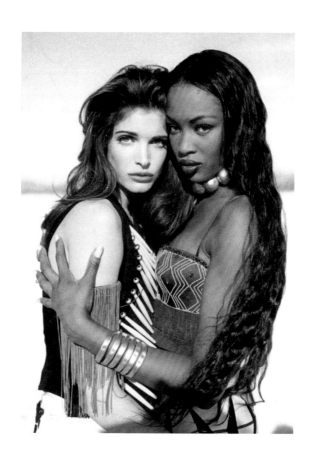

Naomi Campbell, Stephanie Seymour

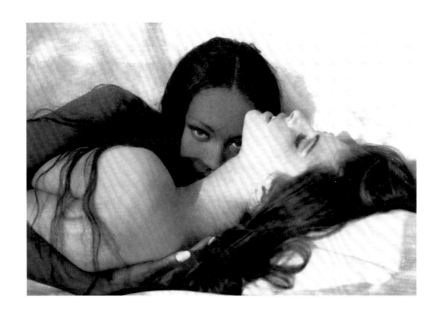

Naomi Campbell, Stephanie Seymour

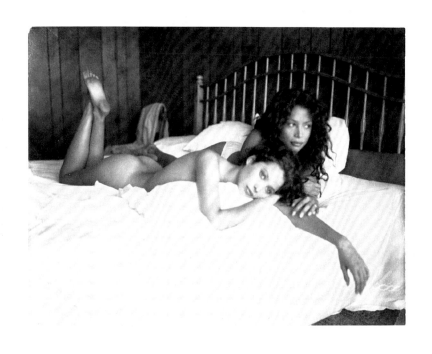

Christy Turlington, Kara Young

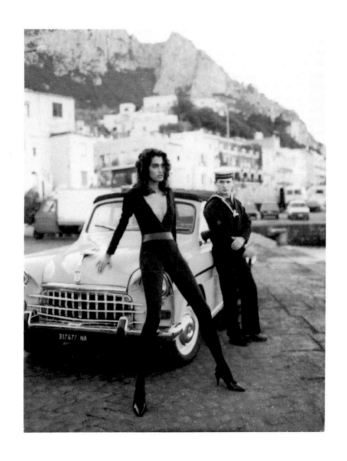

Yasmeen Ghauri

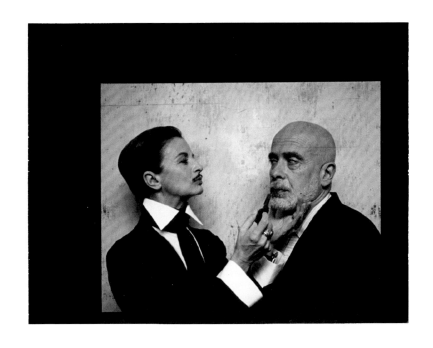

Alba & Francesco Clemente

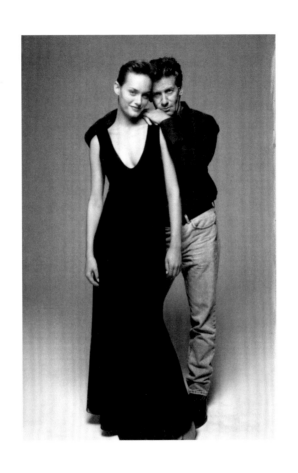

Calvin Klein, Amber Valletta

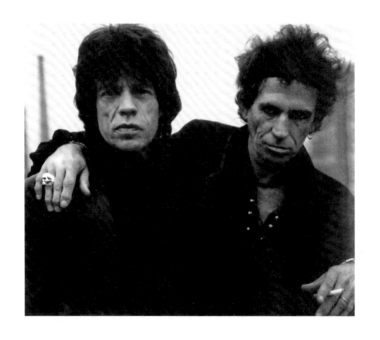

Mick Jagger, Keith Richards

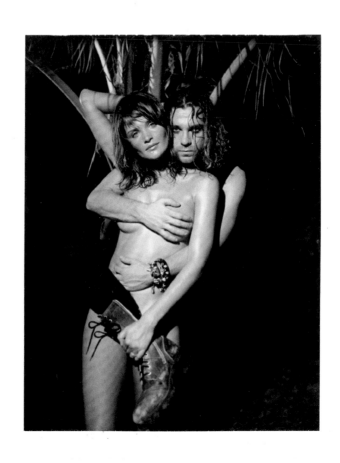

Helena Christensen, Michael Hutchence

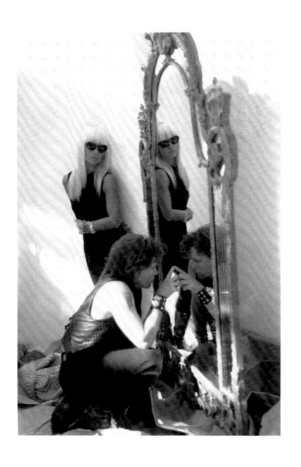

Donatella Versace, Jon Bon Jovi

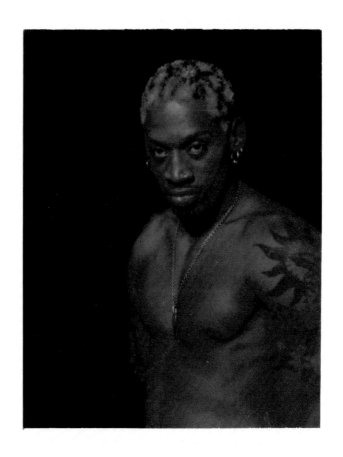

Dennis Rodman

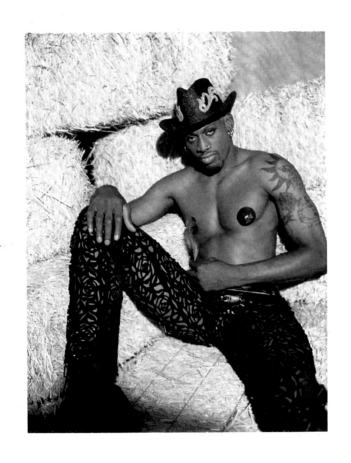

Dennis Rodman

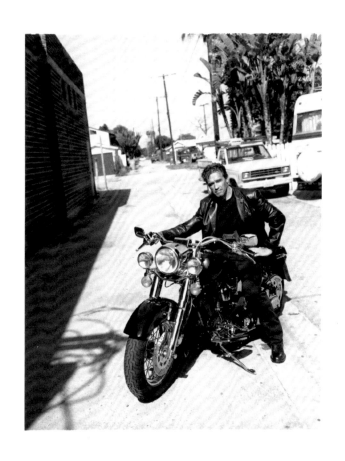

Arnold Schwarzenegger

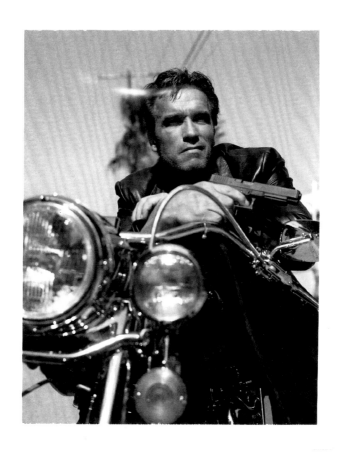

Arnold Schwarzenegger

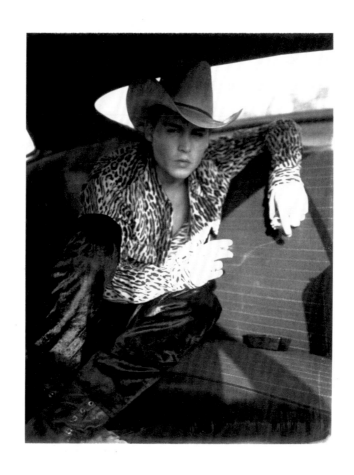

Johnny Depp

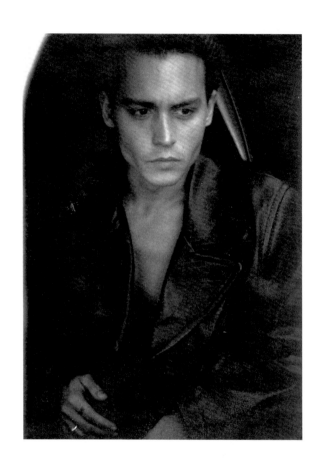

Johnny Depp

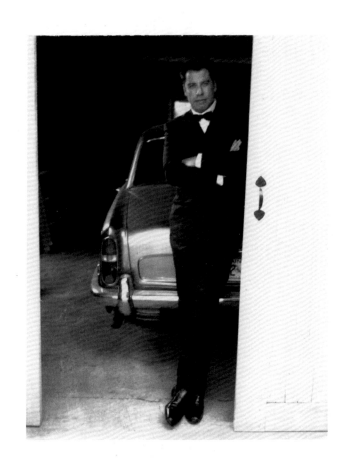

John Travolta

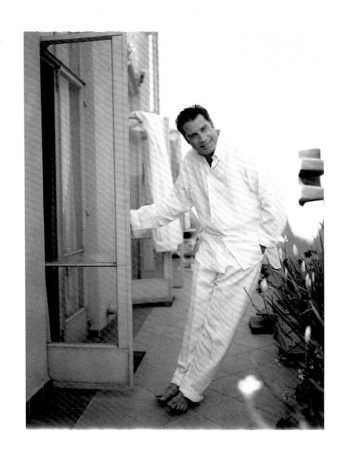

John Travolta

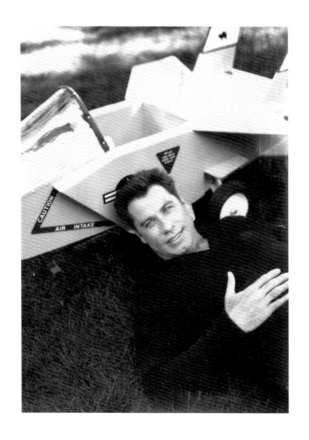

John Travolta

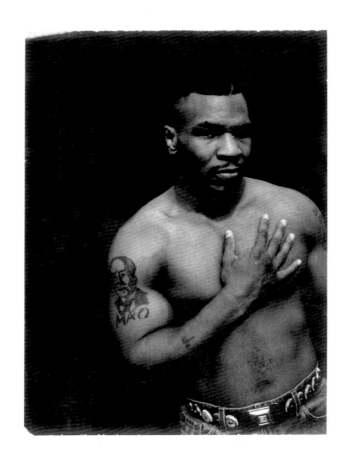

Mike Tyson

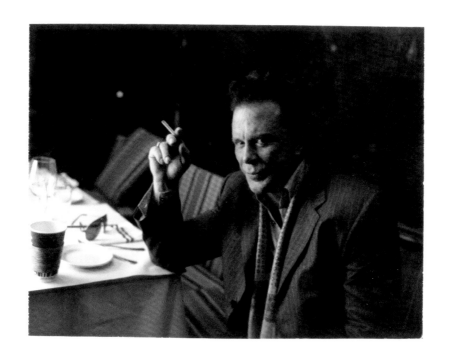

Mickey Rourke

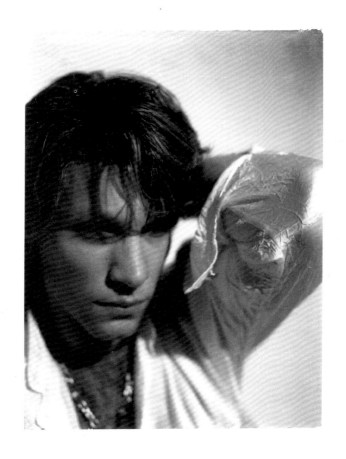

Jon Bon Jovi

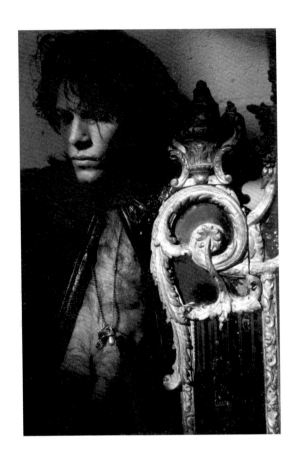

Jon Bon Jovi

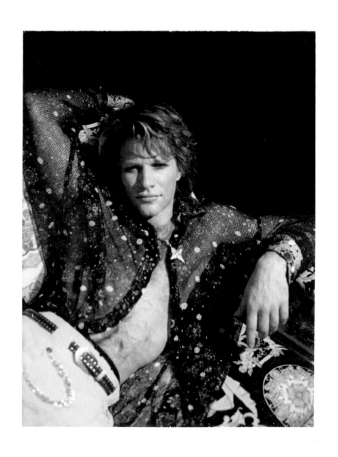

Jon Bon Jovi

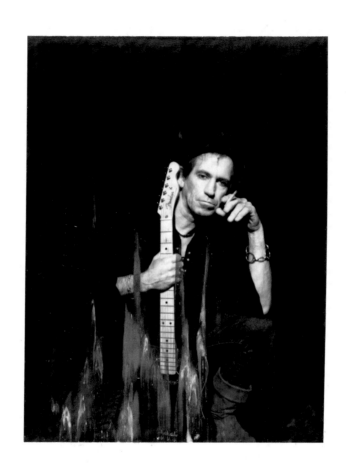

Keith Richards

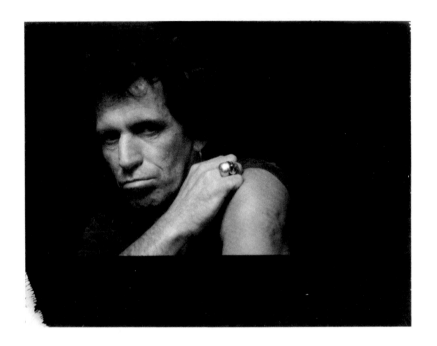

Keith Richards

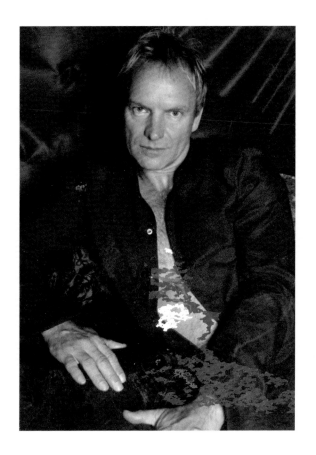

Sting

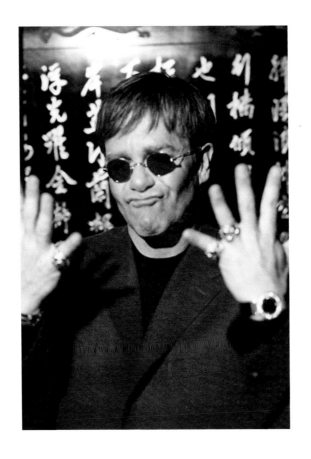

Elton John

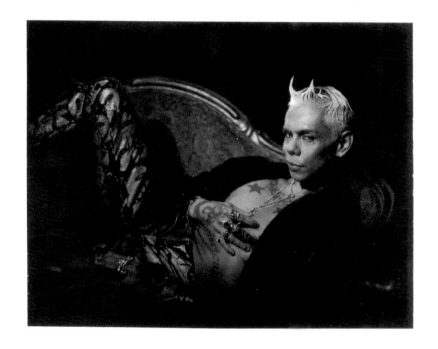

Raven O

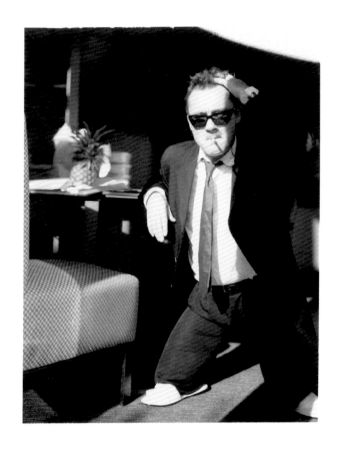

Damien Hirst

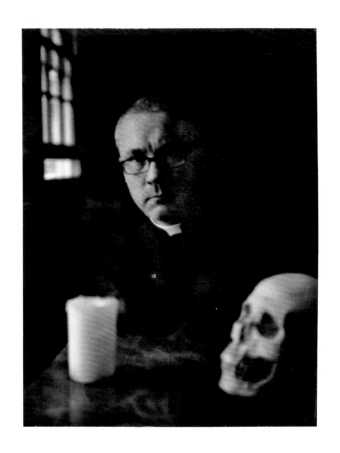

Damien Hirst

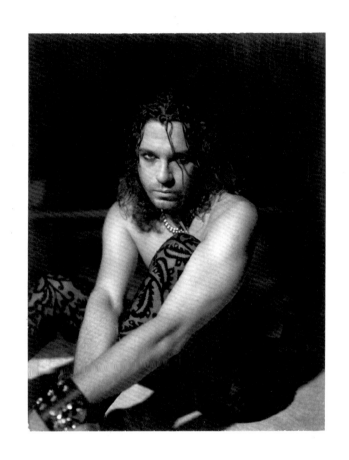

Michael Hutchence

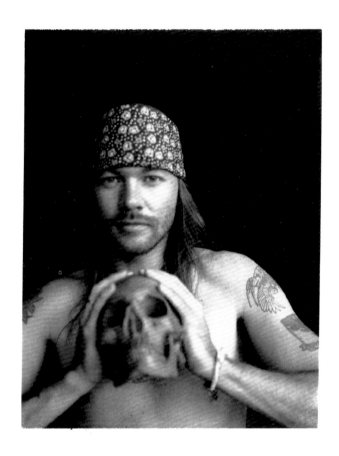

Axl Rose

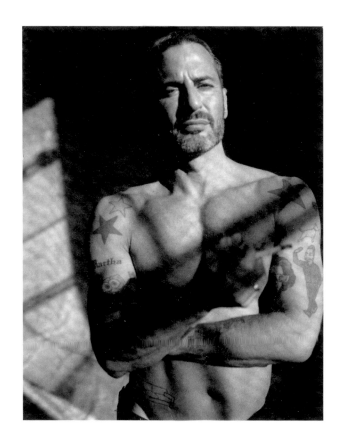

Marc Jacobs

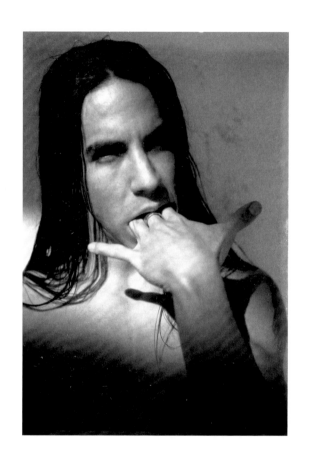

Anthony Kiedis

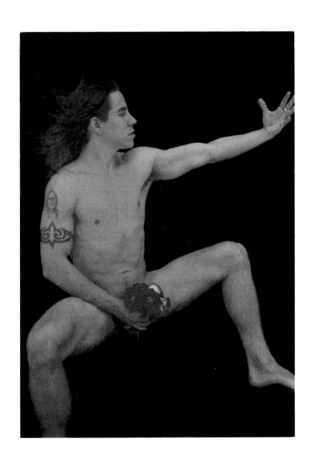

Anthony Kiedis

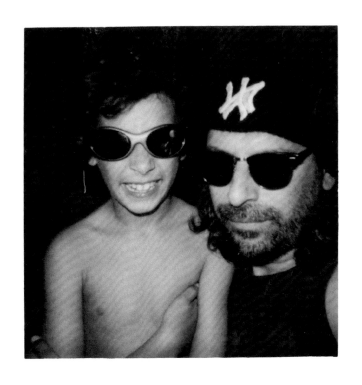

Nick, Sante D'Orazio

Translation into German
by Marion Kagerer

Translation into French
by Martine Passelaigue

Separations, printing and binding: EBS, Verona

ISBN 978-3-8296-0720-9

A Schirmer/Mosel Production
www.schirmer-mosel.com